Sunday Club

New Pitsligo

Parish Church

The illustrations in this book were selected from
My Own Book of Bible Stories, published by Lion Publishing

Text by Lois Rock
Illustrations copyright © 1993 Carolyn Cox
This edition copyright © 2002 Lion Publishing

The moral rights of the author and illustrator
have been asserted

Published by
Lion Publishing plc
Mayfield House, 256 Banbury Road,
Oxford OX2 7DH, England
www.lion-publishing.co.uk
ISBN 0 7459 4633 X

First edition 2002
10 9 8 7 6 5 4 3 2 1 0

A catalogue record for this book is available
from the British Library

Typeset in 13/18 Baskerville MT Schoolbook
Printed and bound in Malaysia

My Book of
Bible
Stories

Retold by Lois Rock
Illustrated by Carolyn Cox

LION
Children's Books

Contents

The
Old Testament

The
New Testament

God Makes the World

In the very beginning, there was nothing – a huge dark nothing like a dark and stormy sea.

God spoke into the nothing: 'Let there be light.' At once, the light shone. God called the light 'Day' and the dark 'Night'. That was the first day.

Then God said, 'Let there be space around the world.' God called the space 'Sky'. That was the second day.

Then God said, 'Let the water come together so land will appear.' The water flowed into deep green pools and the brown land emerged. God called the water 'Sea' and the land 'Earth'.

God spoke again: 'Let the earth produce all kinds of plants.' Soon there were shy seedlings and bright flowers, nodding grasses and tall trees. God was pleased with all that had been made as the third day ended.

The
Old Testament

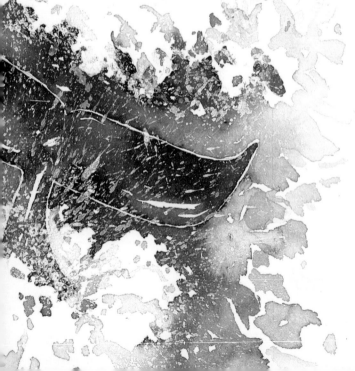

11

Then God said, 'Let there be lights in the sky: the sun for the day, and the moon and stars for the night.' The sun set on God's good world, and the fourth day ended.

Then God said, 'Let there be fish in the sea and birds in the air.' And so it was, and the fifth day ended with the sound of birdsong.

Then God said, 'Let the world be filled with animals.' There were animals of every kind: lumbering hippopotamuses and tiny shrews, graceful gazelles and yawning lions. God smiled. 'And now, let us make human beings to take care of everything that has been made.' God created man and woman and blessed them: 'May you have children, and may you feel at home in the

world. Everything in this world is for you to enjoy.'
That was the sixth day.

In this way, the whole wide world was made.
On the seventh day God rested, and God said that
each seventh day was to be a time for rest and
enjoyment for evermore.

The Garden of Eden

God planted a garden in Eden. It was a beautiful place, watered by a rippling river and shaded by green trees that bowed under the weight of their ripening fruit.

God put the first man, Adam, in the garden, to take care of it. Adam knew all the animals by name, but his only true friend and companion was the first woman, Eve.

In the middle of the garden stood a special tree. Its fruit gave knowledge: knowledge of what is good and what is bad.

'You must not eat from that tree,' warned God. 'If you do, you will die.'

Adam and Eve were perfectly happy in their paradise garden. Then, one day, a snake came slithering by.

'I've heard a whisper,' said the snake to the woman, 'that you're not allowed to eat from all the trees here.'

'Oh yes we are,' said Eve. 'Only one is forbidden; if we eat its fruit we will die.'

'Stuff and nonsense,' simpered the snake. 'It will make you wise. God must be afraid you'll get too wise. Try some.'

Eve wondered. The fruit did look lovely.
So she ate a little and gave some to Adam.

16

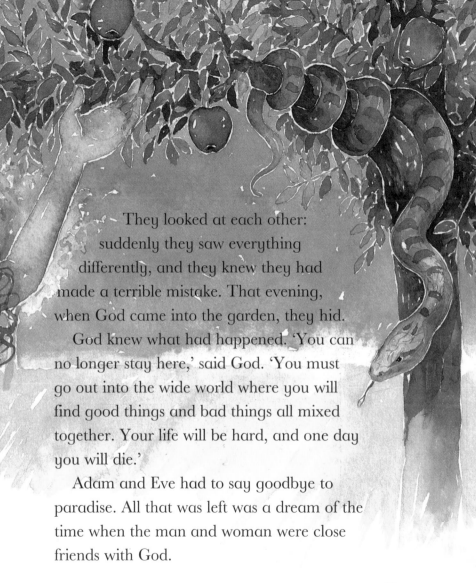

They looked at each other:
suddenly they saw everything
differently, and they knew they had
made a terrible mistake. That evening,
when God came into the garden, they hid.

God knew what had happened. 'You can
no longer stay here,' said God. 'You must
go out into the wide world where you will
find good things and bad things all mixed
together. Your life will be hard, and one day
you will die.'

Adam and Eve had to say goodbye to
paradise. All that was left was a dream of the
time when the man and woman were close
friends with God.

Noah and the Ark

Old man Noah sighed. 'Everywhere I go I see people doing the most wicked things,' he said. 'My three sons will have their own families soon; what kind of world will my grandchildren have to grow up in?'

Then God spoke to him: 'Noah, the world has become so bad that I am going to end it. I am going to send a flood; but you are a good man, and I am going to put you in charge of the new beginning.'

'Whatever shall I do?' asked Noah.

'Build a boat,' said God, 'the Ark. Make it big

enough for you and your family and a pair of
every kind of animal. Take enough food to last
a long time. I will keep you safe.'

Noah did as God said. As the rain began to
fall, Noah led everyone safely onto his boat.

It rained for days and days. It rained so much
that even the highest mountains disappeared. In
all the world there was nothing left but Noah and
his boat.

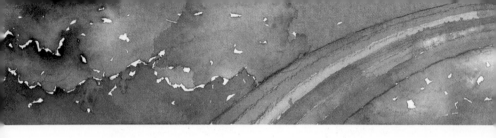

Then, one day, the Ark became stuck. 'We've hit land,' announced Noah.

Soon he could see mountain tops all around. He sent out a raven in search of land, and then a dove. The second time he let the dove fly, it brought back a fresh green leaf.

'Time to go and begin the world all over again,' cried Noah. The animals leaped and ran and scurried and scuttled into the world to make new homes for themselves.

'The animals will have young,' said God, 'and you will have grandchildren.'

Noah and his family gave thanks to God for keeping them safe.

'I am making you a promise,' said God. 'Never again will I flood the world. Look at the rainbow: it is a sign that, for as long as the world exists, there will always be summer and winter, springtime and harvest.'

Abraham and the Promise

'So I have become wealthy,' said Abraham to himself. 'That's what everyone in this town says. I have sheep and goats and camels and cattle, and they think that matters.'

Abraham sighed. He was wealthy. He had a beautiful wife, Sarah; but he had no son, and without a son everything else seemed worthless.

Then God spoke to him: 'I want you to go from here to a new land. It will be a land for your son, and for his children and their children, and for their children's children for ever. I will bless you, and your family will bring my blessing to all the world.'

Abraham was full of hope. He went with all his household to the land of Canaan. There they lived as nomads, always on the move in search of pasture and water for their flocks.

But the years went by, and still Abraham and Sarah had no son. Abraham sat outside in the cool of the night and wondered.

'Look at the sky,' said God. 'Your children's children will be as many as the stars in the sky.

'Look at the earth. Your children's children will be as many as the grains of sand.'

Still nothing happened. Then, one day, three mysterious travellers came by. As the men sat with Abraham eating a meal, they asked about his wife. 'Nine months from now she will have a son,' they said.

Sarah was listening nearby. 'Dear me!' she laughed. 'Don't those men know anything? An old woman like me can't have children. And Abraham's an old man!'

But the strangers' message was from God. Nine months later, Sarah had a son, Isaac. As the boy grew, Abraham learned more and more to have faith in God and in God's promises.

25

Joseph and the Wonderful Coat

Joseph was very proud of himself. He was wearing the wonderful new coat his father Jacob had given him. 'It's not just a coat,' he said to himself, 'more a promise that I'm the most important son in the family. Me! I'm the great grandson of Abraham, the grandson of Isaac, and the much-loved son of Jacob and his favourite wife, Rachel.'

Joseph had ten older brothers who were the sons of their father's other wife, Leah. They hated Joseph. The only brother Joseph got on with was his baby brother, Benjamin.

Joseph seemed to want to make everyone jealous. 'Listen to this,' he said. 'I had a dream. We were in the fields tying up sheaves of wheat. Then my sheaf stood up and your sheaves bowed down to it. What do you make of that?'

The brothers scowled.

Another time he said, 'I had another dream. The sun, the moon and eleven stars bowed down to me.' That even made his father angry. 'Don't dare to think that your whole family is going to worship you!'

But while the ten older brothers had to work hard looking after the sheep, Joseph stayed at home. One day, Jacob sent Joseph to see how the brothers were getting on.

'Here's our chance,' they said. 'Let's get rid of him.' In a moment of anger they planned to kill Joseph.

'Wait! I've a cleverer idea,' said one. 'Let's sell him to those traders I can see over there. They must be going to Egypt. Joseph will fetch a good price as a slave.'

The brothers sold him. They kept the wonderful coat and deliberately stained it with blood. They let Jacob believe that Joseph had been killed by a wild animal.

Jacob wept. Far away in Egypt, Joseph knew that his proud boasting had come to nothing.

Joseph and the Great Famine

'I never dreamed I'd be a slave,' said Joseph to himself. 'But even when that happened I tried to serve my master well. Now his wife has told lies about me, and I'm stuck here in jail with the cockroaches.'

Life was hard. But Joseph had a special talent: he could explain the meaning of dreams. For that, the other prisoners came to like him.

One day, in the palace, the king of Egypt had a dream that no one else could explain. Someone at court knew about Joseph. He was brought from jail to the king.

'Here is my dream,' said the king. 'I saw seven fat cows grazing, and

31

then seven thin cows came and ate them. Then I saw seven plump ears of corn, but seven shrivelled ears of corn came and ate them.'

Joseph explained. 'This is what your dream means: there will be seven years of plenty, with good harvests; then there will be seven years of famine, with bad harvests. You must find someone to take charge and store grain from the seven good years to last the seven bad years.'

The king chose Joseph. He became the second most important person in all of Egypt.

After seven good years, there were bad harvests everywhere. Far away, Joseph's family were

hungry. They heard that there was food in Egypt,
and Joseph's older brothers came to buy some.

Humble and trembling, they bowed down to
the man in charge of the food stores. They didn't
know that it was Joseph.

Joseph recognized them. His heart was
breaking. He knew that he wanted to be friends
with his family again, and especially with his
younger brother, Benjamin.

In the end, Joseph said who he was.

'Let's forget the past,' said Joseph. 'God was
taking care of us all the time. God sent me to Egypt
ahead of you, so I could take care of you now.'

He invited all his family to come to Egypt.
There, they were safe for many years.

The Baby in the Rushes

Little Miriam loved her new baby brother. But her mother had been crying and crying ever since he was born.

'It's not safe for a baby boy here in Egypt,' her mother explained. 'Our people came here hundreds of years ago, when there was no food in our own land. We were welcome then, but the man who is king now only wants us as slaves. He even wants all our baby boys to be thrown into the river.'

Miriam helped to hide the baby. As he grew bigger and noisier, the mother and daughter had to make a clever plan.

They took a basket and covered it with tar to make it waterproof, so it floated. Then they put the baby inside and hid him among the rushes at the edge of the river.

Miriam stayed close by to see what would
happen. The princess of Egypt came down to the
river to bathe. She saw the basket and she
asked her servants to fetch it.

'Oh, a baby!' she cried. 'It must be one of
the slave babies and someone's trying to save
him. I want to rescue him too.'

Miriam stepped forward. 'Would you like someone to look after him for you?' she asked.

'Yes please,' said the princess. Miriam went to fetch her mother. The princess asked her to look after the baby until he was old enough to come and live as a prince in the palace.

'I shall call the baby "Moses",' said the princess. 'It is a name with a special meaning for me, to remind me of how I pulled him out of the water – and out of danger.'

The Great Escape

Moses grew up as an Egyptian prince, but he knew he was really one of the slave people.

One day, when he was grown up, he saw a slave being badly treated by a slave master. Moses was so angry he killed the slave master. That meant that he was in trouble, and he had to run for his life.

In the faraway wilderness he became a shepherd. One day, he saw a strange sight: a bush was covered with flames, but none of it was burning. He heard a voice speaking – it was the voice of God.

God told Moses to go and rescue his people. He must tell the king of Egypt to let them go free.

'I won't be any good at that,' Moses argued. 'I'm not good at talking.'

'I will help you,' said God, 'and you can ask your brother, Aaron, to help you too.'

Moses did as God wanted. For a long time, the king said no. He did not want to let his slaves go free.

'God has told me that there will be disaster after disaster if you don't,' warned Moses. What Moses said came true. First the river turned blood red. Next came an invasion of frogs; then gnats, then flies. The animals died, and then the people fell ill. There were hailstorms; and great clouds of locusts flew in from the wilderness. Three long days were as dark as night.

The final disaster was the worst: the eldest son in every house in Egypt died. Amid the

sound of weeping, only the slave people were
safe. God was taking special care of them.

At last the king said that Moses could take the
people away. God led them through a marshy
sea. When the king suddenly panicked and sent
soldiers in chariots to fetch everyone back, the
same marshes stopped them in their tracks.

'God has set us free,' cheered the people. It
was a new beginning.

The Golden Box

Moses led his people out of Egypt. 'God will take us to the good land of Canaan, where we can make our home,' he told them.

The journey was long, and the wilderness was a dry and dusty place.

The people began to complain. 'We were better off in Egypt,' they moaned.

'God will take care of us,' promised Moses.

It was true. God helped Moses to find clean water for them to drink. God sent food called manna, which they gathered like flakes of frost, and plump birds called quails, which were easy to catch and good to eat.

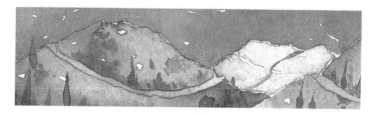

Even so, the people were not happy. They were
scared of going to Canaan, for other peoples
already lived there.

Instead they spent years in the wilderness. In
that time, Moses taught them how to live as
God's people.

'You must love God more than
anything,' said Moses, 'and you must
treat other people as kindly as you want
to be treated.

'You must worship God respectfully,' said Moses. 'As we travel, we have tents to live in. We must make a special tent for God, and it will remind us that God is with us.'

The tent was made of the finest materials and hung with curtains of blue and purple and red. The furnishings were made of gold. At the very heart was a golden box, and in the box was a copy of God's laws.

'The box is the sign of God's promise to us,' said Moses. 'God is our God, and we are God's people.'

The years went by. The people slowly began to understand how to obey God.

'I am old now,' said Moses, 'too old to go to the new land. Brave Joshua will lead you there, and you will find out that you really can trust in God.'

Joshua and the Battle of Jericho

'Look,' said Joshua to the people. 'Over there is the land where God has said we can make our home.'

It was a good land, but the people were worried. There were still other nations living there. How were they going to claim land for themselves?

Fortunately, their leader, Joshua, was a brave soldier, and he was also someone who kept God's laws.

'First we must cross the River Jordan,' he said. 'The priests will go first into the water, carrying the golden box that is the sign of God's promise. When they are standing in the water, God will make a way for all of us.'

By a miracle, the river dried to a trickle and everyone crossed safely into the land of Canaan. They came to the first city: Jericho, surrounded by high walls and defended by soldiers.

'God will help us take the city,' said Joshua. Every day for six days, the people marched round Jericho. Soldiers led the way; then came priests blowing trumpets, and more priests carrying the golden box. Behind them came the army.

The people inside Jericho grew more and more afraid. Was the army ever going to attack?

On the seventh day the same thing happened… only this time Joshua's people marched round a second time, then a third, and a fourth, and a fifth and a sixth and a seventh time.

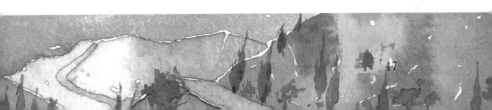

'God has given you the city,' shouted Joshua to his soldiers. They gave a great shout, the priests blew their trumpets, and the walls fell down.

Joshua won the city of Jericho that day. Then he led the people further into the land. Sometimes they had to fight, but other times they made friends with the people they met in the new land and told them more about their God and the good laws they lived by.

When Joshua was old and the land was their home, he called everyone together. 'I and my family choose to live as God wants,' he declared. 'What will you do?'

'We promise to live as God wants,' the people all replied.

49

Samuel Hears a Voice

In a place called Shiloh, there was a special tent
set aside for the worship of God. In the tent, the
priests watched over a golden box: the special box
that was a sign of God's promise to look after
the people. Every year, people made a special
journey to come and worship God there.

One year, Hannah came with her husband.
She was very unhappy because she did not have
any children. At Shiloh, she prayed to God, and
she promised that if only she could have a son
she would give him back to God, to serve God
all his life.

By the next year, she had a baby, Samuel. When he was old enough, Hannah brought him to Shiloh to live there and help the priests.

Old Eli took care of Samuel. One night, Samuel was sleeping in God's tent when he heard a voice calling him.

He jumped up and ran to Eli. 'Here I am,' he said.

Eli was puzzled. 'I didn't call you,' he said. 'Go back to bed.'

A second time Samuel heard a voice and once again he ran to Eli.

'I didn't call,' said Eli. 'Go back to bed.'

The same thing happened a third time. Then Eli understood. 'Go back to bed,' he said. 'If you hear the voice again, say this: "Speak, Lord, for I am listening."'

God did speak to Samuel that night. The message was sad news for Eli: his sons were wicked, and God did not want them to serve him. Instead, God had chosen Samuel to be his servant.

God often spoke to Samuel, and Samuel grew wise. He became a great leader of his people and helped them to live as God's people should.

Samuel the Kingmaker

When Samuel grew old, the people came to tell him about their worries.

'The nations who live all around us have kings,' they said. 'We want a king to be our leader.'

Samuel shook his head sadly. 'Kings always end up treating their people like slaves,' he warned, but the people did not want to listen.

Samuel told God about the problem, and God told Samuel to let them have their way.

God also showed Samuel who to choose to be the people's first king – a handsome young man named Saul. At first Saul did well. He listened to Samuel's wise advice, he obeyed God and fought bravely.

Then he began to go his own way. He began to think he knew better than Samuel. God told Samuel that it was already time to choose the next king.

Samuel listened to what God said and then
set off for the town of Bethlehem. There, he went
to the house of a man named Jesse. 'I would like
to see your sons,' Samuel said to Jesse.

One by one the young men came to meet
Samuel. Samuel grew puzzled. None of them
was God's choice. Had he made a mistake in
coming here?

'Haven't you got any more sons?' asked
Samuel, almost ready to give up.

'There's just one,' said Jesse, 'but he's only
a boy. He's out looking after the sheep.'

Samuel asked to see him. Young David strode
in, singing noisily and twanging a harp. 'This is
the one,' Samuel thought.

He performed the ceremony of anointing with
oil to show that David was God's chosen king.

'You will not be king at once,' said Samuel. 'Not till after Saul.'

David smiled. He had grown up knowing about God and loving God, and now God had chosen him.

David and Goliath

King Saul frowned. The war against the Philistines was going badly. They were brave and cunning, and had strong iron weapons.

Saul's army were worried. They did not seem to be able to win. They had few weapons, and even those they had weren't very strong.

They all looked towards the Philistine army camped on the opposite hill.

As they watched, a giant man strode out. His helmet glittered in the sun and he carried a huge spear. Beside him was another soldier carrying a heavy shield with which to protect his master.

'I am Goliath,' roared the giant. 'Come and fight me. If you can find someone to beat me, then you will win, and we will go away. But if not...'

Saul's army shuddered with fear. Goliath's mocking laugh rang across the hills.

One day, David came to visit his brothers who were in Saul's army. Goliath came out and gave the challenge, as he did every day.

'How dare that Goliath think he can beat us!' said David. 'God is our helper.'

David's brothers thought he was simply being cheeky, but David really wanted to fight Goliath. When King Saul heard, he offered him his armour.

'It's too heavy,' said David. 'I know how to fight without that.'

He took his shepherd's stick and a sling that he used to hurl stones. Then he sauntered down towards Goliath, stopping to choose five pebbles.

'How dare you come to fight me like that?' roared Goliath.

'I dare because I trust in God,' replied David. At that, he took a stone and hurled it at the giant. Goliath fell.

Behind him, the army cheered. David had won! He was a hero!

Fearless King David

'David is our hero! He has beaten our enemies!'
The people shouted and danced for joy.

King Saul should have been pleased, and in a
way he was, but he was also very jealous.

'What if David tries to make himself king?' he
worried. 'What will happen to me? What will
happen to my son Jonathan?'

In fact, David and Jonathan had become best
friends. When Saul, in a dark mood, made a plot
to kill David, Jonathan helped him to escape.

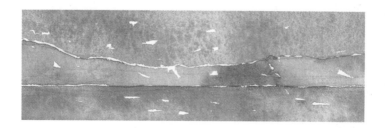

David became an outlaw, living with a band of friends in the wilderness. Saul was desperate to find him and get rid of him, but God kept David safe.

All the time, the people's enemies, the Philistines, were watching. With David out of the army, they began to attack Saul and his men. In a great battle, Saul and Jonathan were both killed.

David wept for the friend he loved and the king he admired, but he knew that his time had come. He began to drive out his people's enemies. He captured a city on a hill and made it his own – the city of Jerusalem.

'This will be God's city,' he said. He arranged
for the golden box that was the sign of God's
promise to be brought into Jerusalem, and there
was great rejoicing.

'I shall build a temple for God here,' thought
David. When the people had lived in tents, it had

been right to have a tent for God. Now that they had homes and a homeland that was safe from enemies, they wanted a proper home for God.

'That is not for you to do,' God told him. King David's job had been to lead his people to victory and to peace.

65

Wise King Solomon

David's son Solomon became king after him. He was a young man, and the job of being king seemed very hard.

One night, in a dream, God asked him what he would want if he could have just one thing.

'I would want to be wise,' said Solomon. 'That is what I most need to rule your people well.'

Solomon did become wise. He became famous for the clever way he helped his people to settle their quarrels. He was famous for his wise sayings.

He also knew how to make good plans. He put himself in charge of building a temple for God – a temple of strong stone, carved cedarwood and the finest gold. The gold box that was a sign of God's promise was brought there, and priests led the people in worship.

In a land far away, the Queen of Sheba heard of Solomon's kingdom, of his wealth and his wisdom. She came with her servants and her camels and rich gifts. She came with the hardest questions she could think of, to test if Solomon was wise.

What she saw was even more marvellous than she had imagined. 'Truly,' she exclaimed, 'your God is good to you.'

For ever after, people remembered the time of Solomon as a time of gold.

Elijah and the Fire

Elijah sighed. If only he had been born in the time of King Solomon, when everyone worshipped God in the temple in Jerusalem.

Now the people were divided, north and south. In the north, King Ahab cared nothing for God. He worshipped Baal.

Elijah was God's prophet. 'Take a message to Ahab,' said God. 'Tell him there will be no rain until I say so. Then he will know who is God.'

Elijah did so. Then, as God had warned, the land dried out. God kept Elijah safe by a little brook, where ravens brought him food. Then, even the brook dried up. God led Elijah to the home of a poor woman and her son. By a miracle, God provided enough food for the little household all through the famine.

In his palace, King Ahab grew worried. Was it ever going to rain again?

At last, Elijah came back.

'Here comes trouble,' snarled Ahab.

'You are the cause of the trouble,' said Elijah. 'But now you are going to find out who is God.'

Elijah told the king to bring the prophets of Baal to a mountain for a contest in front of all the people.

First the prophets of Baal prepared an altar and laid their sacrifice on it. Then they called to Baal to set it alight. Nothing happened, and nothing happened. They called some more, and still nothing happened.

Then Elijah prepared his sacrifice. He poured water all over the altar till even the ground was soaked.

Then he said a prayer: 'Lord God, show that you are our God.'

The fire came blazing down onto Elijah's altar. 'The Lord is God,' everyone shouted.

That night, the rain came.

The Story of Jonah

Once upon a time there lived a man named Jonah. One day, God spoke to him: 'Jonah, I want you to go the city of Nineveh. The people there are very wicked. You must tell them to change their ways. If they don't, I will destroy them.'

Jonah did not want to go. He ran away and got on a boat that was going far, far away.

When the boat was at sea, a storm began to blow. The sailors were terrified.

'God must be punishing us,' cried the sailors. 'Someone here must have made God angry.'

Jonah had to tell the truth. 'I'm the one to blame,' he said. 'Throw me overboard or we'll all die.'

The sailors didn't want to harm Jonah, but the storm got worse. So they said a

prayer and threw him into the sea.

Jonah thought he was about to drown, but a big fish came and swallowed him. Inside the fish, Jonah had time to think. 'I'm sorry, God,' he said. 'I will always obey you from now on.'

The fish took Jonah to land and spat him onto a beach. Jonah hurried off to Nineveh.

'Change your wicked ways,' cried Jonah, 'or God will punish you.'

The people listened. The king listened. The king ordered everyone to say sorry to God.

Jonah was cross. 'The people of Nineveh deserved to be punished,' he muttered to God. 'You're too forgiving. It's not fair.'

Jonah sat and sulked. He sulked in the sun. He sulked in the shade. He sulked even more when the lovely plant that gave him shade died.

'Everything is so unfair!' he cried.

'Oh, you care about a plant, do you?' said God. 'Well, I care about the people of Nineveh and all their animals.'

The Fiery Furnace

God had given the people a land of their own. God had let them have kings to help protect them against their enemies. But as the years went by, the people and the kings often forgot about God. When they did, it seemed that everything went wrong.

Hundreds of years after the time of Solomon, the great enemy was the king of Babylon. His armies came and captured Jerusalem. Many of the people were taken away to Babylon itself.

One day, the king had a huge golden statue made of one of his gods and ordered everyone to come and see it. They all gathered. 'When my musicians play, everyone is to bow down to my statue,' he declared.

The music played. Everyone bowed down – everyone except Shadrach, Meshach and Abednego.

When the king heard about them, he was furious. 'If you will not worship the great god of Babylon, then you will be thrown into a fiery furnace,' he said.

'Our God can help us,' the three men replied. 'In any case, we won't worship your god.'

The king ordered the fire to be made seven times hotter than usual. Shadrach, Meshach and Abednego were bound hand and foot and flung into the flames.

The king looked to see his punishment working. He gasped: he could see four men walking in the flames, and one of them looked like an angel.

'Shadrach! Meshach! Abednego! Come out!' he ordered.

The men walked out. They were not burned; they were not singed. They didn't even smell of smoke.

'Their God sent an angel to rescue them,' said the king. 'Their God is a great God. I therefore order that no one is to say a word against the God of Shadrach, Meshach and Abednego.'

Daniel and the Lions

Daniel was loyal to God. Three times every day he went to the window that looked towards Jerusalem and said his prayers.

Daniel was also the best servant a king could have. Daniel had been a wise helper to the king of Babylon. When that king was beaten by the Persians, Daniel became the most important official in the court of King Darius of Persia.

The other officials were jealous of Daniel. They made a plan and went to see the king.

'O king, live for ever,' they said. 'We have agreed a new law. For thirty days, no one in your kingdom is to ask for anything from anyone, man or god, except yourself. Anyone who disobeys must be thrown to the lions.'

King Darius was pleased. It was a law to find out who was loyal and to get rid of anyone who wasn't. 'This is my law and it must not be broken,' he declared.

Then the men went to spy on Daniel. As soon as they saw him saying prayers to God, they rushed to tell the king.

'Your majesty,' they said. 'You made a new law that, for thirty days, anyone who asked for anything from any man or god except you should be thrown to the lions.'

'That is true,' replied the king. 'The law of Persia cannot be changed.'

Then the men said, 'Daniel does not respect you or your law. He prays to his God three times a day.'

Darius was most displeased. He did not want to get rid of his finest official, but his law was law.

Daniel was marched to the pit of lions. 'May your God help you,' whispered Darius. Then Daniel was thrown inside and the door was locked.

Darius worried all evening. When the next morning dawned, Darius rushed back to the lion pit.

'Are you still there?' he called to Daniel.

'O king, live for ever,' replied Daniel. 'God knows I have done nothing wrong, and God has kept me safe.'

Darius was overjoyed. Daniel was pulled to safety. 'Now throw Daniel's enemies to the lions,' Darius ordered. 'Everyone is to know that Daniel's God is the living God.'

Nehemiah and the City of Jerusalem

God had promised to give the people a land of their own. When the people had forgotten about God, enemies had taken them far away, and Jerusalem had been destroyed. But God had promised to bring them home again.

The king who ruled them, King Cyrus of Persia, made a proclamation: 'Let God's people return to Jerusalem. Let them rebuild their temple.'

The people were overjoyed, and many went home. To their dismay, they found a ruin, and they wept.

But they were keen to work, and slowly they managed to build a new temple – not as grand as King Solomon's, but a temple all the same.

Back in Persia, Nehemiah still worked for the king. He was eager to hear how his people were getting on with rebuilding Jerusalem. He heard

that the city itself was still tumbledown. It didn't
even have walls. Nehemiah wanted to help.

The king gave him permission to go, and Nehemiah made the journey. He rode his donkey around the city to see what needed to be done.

Then he came up with a plan. Every family was asked to build a length of wall. The plan was a great success.

The foreigners who lived nearby were angry and jealous. They tried to stop the building. Nehemiah arranged for half the people to build while the other half kept watch.

After fifty-two days, the work was complete. Jerusalem was a city with walls.

There was a great celebration. Everyone marched around the city. They sang and played music. Then they gave thanks to God – their God.

The
New Testament

The Baby in the Manger

Mary lived in the little town of Nazareth. It nestled among the hills of Galilee, but the land was all part of the great Roman empire. Not that it mattered much to Mary – she was simply looking forward to getting married to a man named Joseph.

On one particular day, everything began as usual; but everything changed when an angel appeared.

'Mary,' said the angel, 'God has chosen you to be the mother of a baby – God's own son.'

Mary was puzzled. The message was hard to believe, and she didn't really understand it. But she loved God, and she replied, 'I will do as God wants.'

In a dream, an angel told Joseph to take care of Mary and her baby. Months later, when the baby was almost due, Mary and Joseph had to go on a journey together. The Roman emperor wanted to know how many people lived in his empire, so he could make them pay taxes. Everyone had to go to their home town, and so Mary and Joseph went to Bethlehem.

The town was very crowded. The only place where Mary and Joseph could shelter was in a stable for animals.

There, Mary's baby was born. She wrapped him warmly and laid him to sleep in the manger.

Out on the hills nearby, shepherds were looking after their sheep. Suddenly, the sky grew bright. An angel appeared. 'Here is good news for all the world,' said the angel. 'God's special king

has been born in Bethlehem. He is the
Saviour, the Christ. You will find him
snugly wrapped and lying in a manger.'

Then a thousand angels began to sing:
'Glory to God in the highest, and peace on
earth.'

The shepherds hurried to Bethlehem. They
found the baby, just as the angel had said.

The Wise Men
and the Star

Away in the East, there lived some men who studied the stars. One night, they saw a bright new star. They knew at once what it meant.

'It is a sign that a new king has been born,'
they said. 'We must go and find him.'

They made ready for a long journey and
went on their way, always keeping the star
ahead of them.

In time, they came to the city of Jerusalem. It was part of the Roman empire now, but scheming King Herod ruled over day-to-day matters. He had made the city beautiful, with a splendid new temple, but he had little respect for God. He cared only about being king.

He was angry when he heard that travellers had come in search of a new king. He called his advisers.

'Our people are hoping that God will send them a king, a Christ,' he said. 'Do we know where the king will be born?'

'In Bethlehem,' the advisers replied.

King Herod sent for the wise men and told them to go and look in Bethlehem. 'When you have found the king, come and tell me, so I can go and see him too,' he said. He smiled to himself. His wicked plan was to find the baby and kill him.

The wise men followed the star to Bethlehem. There they found Mary and Joseph and the baby Jesus. They offered him rich gifts: gold and frankincense and myrrh.

An angel warned the wise men not to go back to King Herod, but to go home another way.

In a dream, an angel told Joseph to escape with Mary and the baby to Egypt. There they were safe from the wicked king. Only when they heard he was dead did they return to Nazareth.

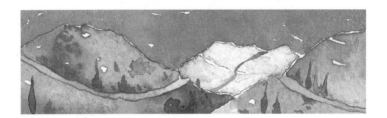

Jesus Grows Up

In the little school in Nazareth, Jesus listened carefully. He wanted to know all about the laws of his people, to learn what was right and what was wrong. He wanted to understand why his people believed that God was going to send a king to lead them to freedom. What sort of king did his teacher think that might be?

The more Jesus learned about God, the more
he wanted to go to the temple in Jerusalem. Every
year, at the time of a festival called Passover, a
group of pilgrims went from Nazareth to the city,
and Mary and Joseph went with them.

When Jesus was twelve, he was allowed to go.
He saw the beautiful temple on the hill, gleaming
in the sunshine. He saw the ceremonies that
celebrated the time, long ago, when God had
chosen Moses to lead his people to freedom. He
saw the hundreds and hundreds of pilgrims, rich
and poor, who had come to worship God from
everywhere.

When the festival was over, the people from
Nazareth set off for home. At twelve, Jesus was
quite grown up, so the group had walked a long
way before Mary wondered where Jesus was.
Who had he been travelling with that day?

No one had seen him. 'This is terrible,' wept Mary. She and Joseph hurried back to Jerusalem.

The next two days they hunted high and low. On the third day they began to fear the worst.

Then, at last, they found Jesus: he was in the temple courtyard, sitting with the teachers, listening to them and asking questions.

'Where have you been? Why have you done this to us?' Mary cried.

Jesus was surprised. 'Surely you knew I had to be in my Father's house!' he replied.

Mary and Joseph did not understand; but Jesus went home with them and was a good and obedient son.

Jesus' New Beginning

Jesus had a cousin named John. When they were both grown up, John became much talked about. He lived out in the wilderness, preaching to anyone who came to listen. 'It's time to get ready to welcome God's chosen king,' he said. 'Give up your bad old ways and make a new start. God will forgive you.'

He baptized those who wanted to change in the River Jordan.

One day, Jesus came along. He asked to be baptized too. 'But you don't need to make a change,' said John. 'You're better than me.'

Jesus insisted. As John lifted him out of the water,
he heard God's voice saying, 'This is my Son.'

After that, Jesus went off by himself in the desert.
He wanted to be alone with God, to think about
all that lay ahead. After forty days without food,
Jesus heard the whisper of temptation: 'You're
God's son. You could turn these stones into bread.'

Jesus had studied the writings of his people: the stories, the laws, the sayings of the prophets. 'No,' he replied. 'The writings say that we need more than bread in order to live.'

The whisperer spoke again: 'You could throw yourself down from the top of the temple. The writings say that God's angels would save you.'

'No,' replied Jesus, 'the writings also say that it

is not right to put God to the test.'

A third time the whisperer spoke: 'You could be king of the whole world. Serve me, and I'll help you...'

'Go away, Evil One,' replied Jesus. 'The writings tell us to serve God alone.'

Then the whisperer went away, and Jesus knew for sure what he must do.

Jesus and the Disciples

Everyone was talking about Jesus. 'Have you heard about the new teacher – the son of Mary from Nazareth? He's going round all the villages talking about God to anyone who will listen.'

'He says that God is welcoming everyone to be part of God's new kingdom, and that everyone must get ready.'

'He's working miracles too. That must mean he's special. He can heal people with just a touch, just a word.'

Jesus made his home in a little town on the shore of Lake Galilee. Among his friends were some of the men who fished the lake from little boats. One day, as he stood on the beach talking to the crowds who had gathered, he saw two boats moored in the shallow water. Jesus got into Peter's boat and asked him to push it further into the lake, so he could speak to the people from there.

Peter went back to washing his nets, but he found himself listening to what Jesus said.

When Jesus had finished talking to the people,

he asked the fishermen to go out a bit further and let their nets down for a catch.

Peter shook his head. 'It's the wrong time of day,' he said. Then he shrugged and did as Jesus had asked.

The nets filled with fish – so many that the nets almost broke as the men hauled them in.

'Leave your fishing,' said Jesus, 'and come and follow me.'

Peter and his brother Andrew, along with two other fishermen, James and John, became Jesus' close friends. Jesus called all kinds of people to follow him – rich and

poor, young and old, men and women.
From them he chose twelve to learn from
him and be his disciples: the four fishermen,
then Matthew the tax collector and Simon,
Philip, Bartholomew, Thomas, James,
Thaddaeus and Judas.

Jesus the Teacher

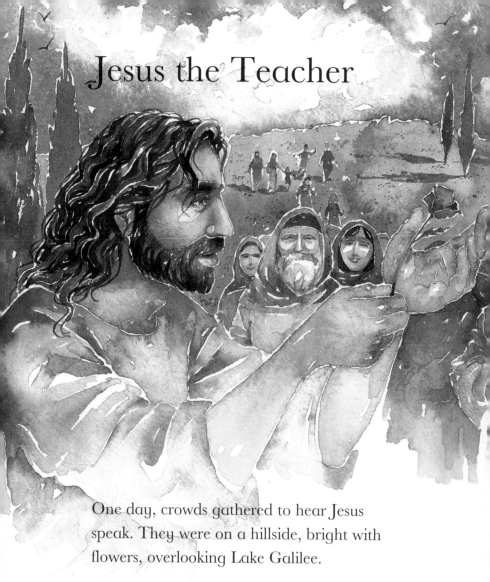

One day, crowds gathered to hear Jesus
speak. They were on a hillside, bright with
flowers, overlooking Lake Galilee.

'Think of all the things you worry about,' said Jesus. 'How will you make a living? Will you ever be rich? Will you always have enough to eat? Will you be able to afford the clothes you need?'

He picked a wild flower. 'Look at the flowers,' he said. 'They don't worry about what to wear. Yet the finery God gives them is more wonderful than even rich King Solomon ever wore.'

He waved towards the birds that fluttered among the bushes. 'Look at the birds. They don't worry about sowing and harvesting and gathering food for the winter. God provides all they need.

'And this is what I want to tell you: make it your aim to live as God wants, to do the things that really matter, the things that will

seem important in heaven. Remember to show love and respect to everyone, even those who hate you. If people treat you badly, forgive them, just like you would want to be forgiven. Do all these things and know that God will take care of you.

'Don't make a big show of doing good things. You may impress other people, but you won't impress God. When you give to someone who is in need, do it quietly, so only you and the person know about it. God will reward you.

'Remember to pray to God,' Jesus said. 'Don't show off about it, as some do. Go into a room alone, or to a quiet place.

'Here is a prayer to use:

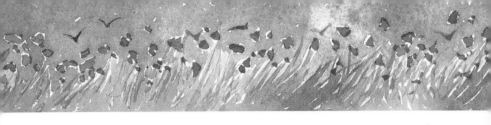

"Our Father in heaven:
May everyone respect your holy name;
may your kingdom come.
May your will be done, on earth as it is in
  heaven.
Give us today the food we need.
Forgive us the wrongs we have done,
as we forgive those who have wronged us.
Do not let hard times come upon us,
and keep us safe from the Evil One.'"

Jesus' followers listened carefully. They wanted to remember all that he said.

Jesus and the Storm

Jesus was tired. He had spent the whole day talking to the crowds and helping those in need. As the sun began to set, he said to his friends, 'Let's take the boat over to the other side of the lake.'

The last of the sunlight sparkled on the water. As the shadows grew darker, Jesus fell asleep in the bottom of the boat.

The boat sailed peacefully across the lake. When it was about halfway, a chilly wind blew down from the hills. The boat began to rock, and the fishermen looked at each other, their faces showing their worry.

'Head for shore, and quickly,' they said, but it was too late. Already the wind was blowing more fiercely, and the waves were tossing the little boat up and down, up and down.

'This is bad, very bad,' muttered Peter. The water was crashing over the side of the boat now, and he was desperately trying to bale it out.

Then the boat dived into the trough of a wave and water poured in.

'Do something! We're going to drown,' shouted someone.

117

Another of the friends shook Jesus awake. 'How can you sleep! Don't you care what's happening!'

Jesus looked around. He saw the waves.

He saw his terrified friends. Then he stood up.

'Be quiet!' he said to the wind.

To the waves he said, 'Lie down now!'

At once the storm was over. The sea was calm, and the air was still.

'Why were you afraid?' asked Jesus. 'Why didn't you trust?'

The friends were really afraid now. Who was this Jesus, who could make the wind and waves do as he told them?

Jesus and the Hungry Crowd

Jesus and his friends were hoping for a restful day. They had taken the boat across the lake to a quiet place on the other side.

'I know where they're going,' someone said. 'We can walk there if we hurry.'

Even as Jesus and his friends arrived they could see hundreds of people rushing to the same place. 'I can't turn them away,' said Jesus. 'I must spend time talking to them.'

And so he did – all through the day, till the shadows grew long.

'You must stop now,' Jesus' friends said to him. 'Send the people to the towns and villages nearby where they can get something to eat.'

'We can't do that,' said Jesus. 'We must give them something.'

121

His friends were puzzled. 'We haven't got the money to feed a crowd,' they said. 'And where would we get food?'

'See who does have food,' said Jesus.

They asked the crowd, and a boy came forward with a small basket. Inside were five loaves and two small fishes.

'Ask everyone to sit down,' said Jesus. Then he took the food, said a prayer of thanks and began to give pieces out to his friends to share with the crowd.

To their amazement, there was enough for everyone. When the meal was over, the disciples gathered twelve baskets of scraps.

The following day, the crowd came back. 'Don't be hungry for the kind of bread you had yesterday,' he said. 'Be hungry for me and my teaching; then you will be satisfied for ever.'

Jesus Heals a Little Girl

The lake shore was as crowded as could be.
Everyone was trying to catch a glimpse of Jesus,
to get close enough to hear his teaching better.

Jairus came hurrying down. 'Excuse me,' he
pleaded, 'can I get through?'

People grudgingly made way for him. After all,
they'd got there first; but Jairus was one of the
community leaders, and that made him quite
important.

Jairus was almost in tears when he reached Jesus. 'My daughter is very ill,' he said, 'and we're afraid she may not get better. Please come and make her well. Please come now.'

Jesus agreed to go with Jairus; but the crowd held him back. Everyone wanted to see him, to ask a question, to touch him. They were only halfway there when messengers came from the man's house and said, 'You need not bother to bring Jesus now; your little girl has died.'

Jesus comforted Jairus. 'Don't worry. Trust me.'

When they reached the house, people were wailing and crying for the little girl.

'Don't make all this noise,' said Jesus. 'The little girl is only sleeping.'

'She is not!' snorted one of the women. 'I've seen dead people, and she's dead.'

Jesus went calmly into the house, allowing just the girl's mother and father and three of his friends to come with him.

He went to where the little girl lay in bed, pale and not breathing. He took her hand. 'Little girl,' he said, 'get up.'

The girl took a breath like a loud sigh, then she sat up.

'Don't tell people about this,' said Jesus to the parents. 'Just give your daughter something to eat and take care of her.'

Jesus' friends were astonished: here was someone who was stronger than death itself.

Jesus' Story of the Lost Sheep

All kinds of people wanted to hear what Jesus had to say and Jesus welcomed them all. Among the crowds there were usually quite a number of not-very-respectable people, and this made some of the others feel quite uncomfortable.

Some of the very religious people began to mutter about the situation. 'If Jesus were really from God, he wouldn't mix with those good-for-nothings,' they said.

Jesus knew what they were thinking. He told this story: 'Imagine that you were a shepherd, with a flock of one hundred sheep. You'd know each one in its own right; you'd know exactly what made each sheep different.

'So imagine how you'd feel if one went missing.'

'You'd go looking for it straight away,' called someone in the crowd.

'Of course you'd go looking for it,' said Jesus. 'You'd leave the ninety-nine in a safe pasture and go out into the hills to search every last dip and gully.

'When you found your lost sheep, you'd pick it up carefully and carry it back home.

'Then, when you'd made the sheepfold safe for the night, you'd gather your friends together for a party,' said Jesus. 'That's how glad you'd be.'

Jesus looked directly at the religious people who had been muttering about him. 'God is like that shepherd,' he said. 'The angels in heaven celebrate when one person who has got their life in a mess changes their ways and comes back home to God.'

Jesus' Story of the Runaway Son

Jesus wanted everyone to know how much God welcomes people. He told this story: 'There was once a man who had two sons. They both worked on the family farm, and they were wealthy.

'The younger son dreamed of more exciting things. He thought of a plan and went to his father. "Half of all this will be mine when you're dead," he said unkindly. "But I want the money now."

'The father was sad. He was sure the young man was making a mistake. Still, he let him have what he wanted and waved him goodbye.

'The son went to a big city, far away. He

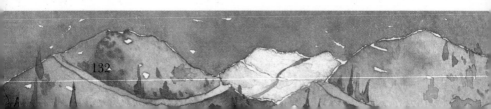

made sure he had a good time – always spending, throwing parties and surrounding himself with good-time friends.

'Then the harvests failed and the price of food went up everywhere. The young man ran out of money. He ran out of food. His friends were nowhere to be seen.

'Desperate and hungry, he took a job looking after pigs.

'"I've been so wrong," he sighed. "I'm even tempted to eat the pig food." Then a thought struck him. "My father's servants live better than this. I shall go home, say how sorry I am and ask to be taken on as a servant there."

'And so he set off for home. But while he was still a long way off, his father saw him coming. He ran to greet him and welcomed him with a big party.

'The older brother heard the noise. When he found out what the party was for, he was cross. "What has my selfish brother done to deserve this?" he complained. "Why don't I get a party?"

'"But everything I have is already yours," his father replied. "We must be happy today. Your brother was as good as dead, but he's come home alive. He was lost, but now he is found."'

Jesus' Story of the Good Samaritan

A man hurried through the crowd to ask Jesus a question. 'Teacher,' he said, 'what must I do to be part of God's everlasting kingdom?'

'What do the laws say?' replied Jesus.

'That I must love God completely and love my neighbour as myself.'

'That's right,' said Jesus.

'But who is my neighbour?' asked the man.

Jesus told a story: 'There was once a man who was travelling from Jerusalem to Jericho. Out in the wild hills, robbers leaped down from their cave and beat him up. They took his money and left him for dead.

'A priest came by. He saw the man and was worried. "What a dreadful thing to happen in this dreadful place," he thought.

'He hurried quickly by, staying as far away from the man as he could.

'Next came a Levite, who worked in the temple. He saw the man and walked right up to him. The man seemed dead. The Levite hurried on by.

'Then came a Samaritan,' said Jesus. Samaritans were foreigners to Jesus' listeners, and there was a lot of bad feeling between the two groups. No one would expect good things from a Samaritan.

Jesus continued his story: 'The Samaritan saw the man. He stopped and went over to him. He cleaned the man's wounds and bandaged them. Then he lifted the man onto his donkey and took him to an inn, where he took care of him.

'The next day he went to the innkeeper, money in hand. "Take care of the man for me," he said.

"If it costs more than I am giving you now, I will pay the extra when I come back this way."

'So the question is this,' said Jesus. 'Who was a neighbour to the man?'

'The one who helped him,' came the answer.

'You go then and do the same,' said Jesus.

The Man in the Tree

The people of Jericho were full of excitement. Jesus was coming to their town. The streets were already crowded, everyone jostling to get a good place.

At the back of the crowd, Zacchaeus was angry. Why had he been born short? He couldn't see a thing!

'Come on, be fair and let me get to the front,' he said bossily. The people turned to look, then turned away. They knew Zacchaeus – the man who'd made himself rich collecting their money in taxes for the Romans. Worse than that, everyone knew he charged too much. That's how tax collectors made their money. And now Zacchaeus wanted to be treated fairly? Not likely.

Zacchaeus was determined to see Jesus. Then he had an idea. He ran to a tree further along the road and climbed up. Now he had a perfect view!

At last, Jesus came along. Then he stopped,

right by the tree. He looked up. 'Come down,
Zacchaeus,' he called. 'I want to come to your
house.'

Zacchaeus was so surprised he nearly fell as he
hurried down. He shut his ears to the muttering:
'Hmmph. Jesus is going to visit that criminal, is
he? To share a meal I suppose, as if they were
friends. I don't think much of that.'

Zacchaeus gave Jesus the warmest welcome.
He listened as Jesus talked with him, and
everything Jesus said made sense. At the
end of the meal he stood up and made an
announcement to everyone in the room.

'I haven't done good things with my life,' he said, 'but now I'm going to change. I'm going to give half my money to the poor, and I'm going to repay those I've cheated four times over.'

Jesus smiled. 'Someone has been saved today. This is why I came: to rescue people from their bad ways and bring them home to God.'

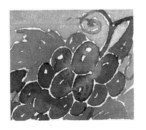

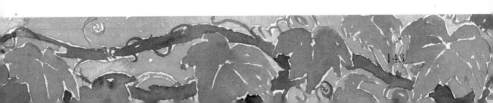

Jesus Rides to Jerusalem

It was a day in the spring. The road to Jerusalem was crowded. People were travelling to the city from everywhere. They all wanted to celebrate the great festival of Passover at the temple.

Suddenly there was a whisper of excitement: 'Look who's coming!'

'It's Jesus! A miracle worker, so they say.'

'Some people are saying more than that! They're hoping he's going to make himself king and set our nation free.'

'Of course! He's riding to the city like a king. Let's give him a royal welcome!'

The crowds started to shout: 'Long live the king! God bless the king.'

Some cut branches from palm trees and waved them like banners. Others flung their cloaks on the ground to make a carpet for Jesus' donkey to walk on.

'Such a nice donkey,' said a little girl.

Her brother stopped cheering for a moment. 'A proper king ought to ride a war horse,' he said. 'People who are going to fight don't ride donkeys.'

'Perhaps Jesus isn't going to fight,' said the girl. 'He heals people. I don't think he wants to hurt people.'

The crowds went on cheering as Jesus went into the city. He went first to the temple. Inside the courtyards there were stalls selling the things people

needed for the festival: animals and birds to give
as an offering to God, and special coins. The
noise was deafening as people argued about
prices. The stallholders were cheating their
customers.

Jesus saw all this and he was very angry. He
tipped up one of the stalls and sent the coins
rolling. Then he began to drive the stallholders
away.

'God says this temple is a house of prayer,' he
said. 'You have made it a den of robbers.'

Some of the religious leaders were very angry.
'There's trouble ahead,' they muttered.

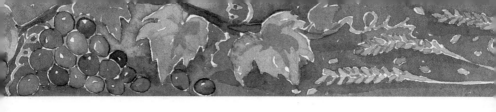

The Darkest Day

Jerusalem was always a lively place at Passover time. The year that Jesus rode in welcomed by a cheering crowd, it was buzzing with excitement. What was he going to do next? Was he going to free the people from their Roman enemies?

The religious leaders were very worried too. Whatever Jesus was planning, they were sure it meant trouble.

Jesus seemed only to want to go on teaching and healing; but Jesus' friend Judas wanted to make something happen. He went to a secret meeting with the religious leaders. They paid him to tip them off about where to find Jesus alone so they could arrest him.

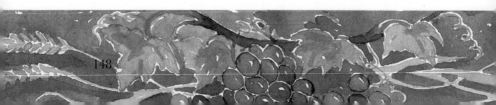

Jesus knew that hard times lay ahead. As he shared the Passover meal with his friends, he broke the bread. 'This is my body,' he said, 'broken for you.'

Later he took the ceremonial cup of wine and shared it round. 'This is my blood,' he said. 'It is spilled for you and for many, to bring you God's forgiveness.'

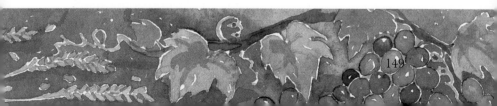

Jesus' friends did not really understand what he was saying. They were glad to go together to a quiet olive grove. While Jesus prayed, they fell asleep.

Then Judas led a band of armed men to arrest Jesus. They took him to the priests, who accused him of all kinds of troublemaking. They took him to the Roman governor, Pontius Pilate, and said he was a dangerous rebel who wanted to make himself his people's king.

Pilate didn't much care. Jesus hadn't done anything to make him worried; but he wanted to keep the leaders of the people happy, so he agreed to have Jesus put to death.

Roman soldiers took Jesus outside the city and crucified him, along with two other criminals.

Jesus hung in great pain. He said a prayer aloud: 'Father, forgive them.' Soon after, he died.

The News that Changed Everything

Jesus' friends were dismayed when he was crucified. They were also frightened for themselves, and they ran away.

A wealthy admirer of Jesus named Joseph went to Pilate and asked to take the body. He had it laid in a stone tomb. As the sun set to mark the beginning of the weekly day of rest, the few who had gathered to help rolled the stone door shut.

The day of rest came and went – a day of great sadness. Early the next morning, some women went back to the tomb to prepare the body in the proper way for burial.

To their amazement, the door of the tomb had been rolled open. Two angels, dressed in white, were sitting there. 'Don't be afraid,' they said. 'Jesus is not here: he is alive. Go and tell all his friends.'

Mary Magdalene stayed behind. She stood by the tomb weeping. The angels spoke to her. 'Why are you crying?' they asked.

'Because they have taken Jesus'
body,' she sobbed. She turned away.
She could see a man among the olive
trees. 'He must be the person who works
here,' she thought. 'Maybe he can help.'

She went to ask him.

The man turned towards her. 'Mary!' he said.

At once she knew: it was Jesus.

The news that Jesus was alive spread among all his friends. They knew it was him. They saw the marks of the nails in his hands and feet. They shared meals together, as they had in the old days.

Yet they knew he was different, too, as he appeared among them even when they were together in a locked room, and disappeared just as suddenly. Jesus had passed through death on to a new kind of life, and his place was now in heaven.

'Go and tell everyone in the world about me and my message,' Jesus told his friends. 'God will give you the help you need.'

A Message for all the World

Jesus had returned to heaven. His friends had seen him go, as if wrapped in a cloud. Now they were puzzled about what to do next.

A few days later, when they were all together indoors, they heard a sound like rushing wind. They saw what looked like tongues of fire dancing over their heads. More than that, they felt brave, as never before – brave enough to tell everyone in the world the whole story of Jesus.

They hurried out into the streets of Jerusalem and began to spread the news. 'Listen to the things that Jesus taught,' they said. 'We know that

his teaching is from God. You saw him put to death on a cross, but we have seen him since then. God has raised him to new life.'

People were curious. They wanted to know more.

157

'This is what it all means,' said one of Jesus' friends. 'God is love. Jesus was God's son. He came to show us just how much God loves us all. He died, as we will all die. God raised him to life, and God wants to welcome us all to new life in God's kingdom as God's friends for ever.

'So let us love God; and let us love one another.'

Many people believed, and their lives were changed.

The news has been spreading ever since – news of love and joy and peace.

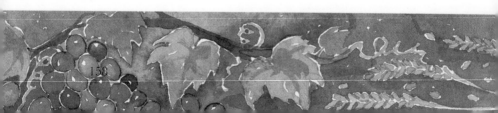